D0761045

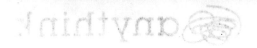

NATIVE AMERICAN BIOGRAPHIES

THE LIFE OF
BLACK ELK

MIRIAM COLEMAN

PowerKiDS press.

New York

Published in 2017 by The Rosen Publishing Group, Inc.
29 East 21st Street, New York, NY 10010

First Edition

Editor: Sarah Machajewski
Book Design: Katelyn Heinle

Photo Credits: Cover (Black Elk) Transcendental Graphics/Archive Photos/Getty Images; cover (landscape) Holly Kuchera/Shutterstock.com; p. 5 Marquette University Archives, Bureau of Catholic Indian Missions Records, ID WBH 01287; p. 7 Joel Sartore/National Geographic/Getty Images; p. 8 https://upload.wikimedia.org/wikipedia/commons/1/16/Custer_Bvt_MG_Geo_A_1865_LC-BH831-365-crop.jpg; p. 9 https://upload.wikimedia.org/wikipedia/commons/b/b2/Charles_Marion_Russell_-_The_Custer_Fight_%281903%29.jpg; p. 10 Kresimir IV/Shutterstock.com; p. 11 Muriel Lasure/Shutterstock.com; p. 13 (main) Buyenlarge/Archive Photos/Getty Images; p. 13 (inset) Marilyn Angel Wynn/Nativestock/Getty Images; pp. 15, 20 courtesy of Library of Congress; p. 17 https://upload.wikimedia.org/wikipedia/commons/0/0a/Black_Elk_and_Elk_of_the_Oglala_Lakota_-1887.jpg; p. 19 https://upload.wikimedia.org/wikipedia/commons/1/13/Ghost_Dance_at_Pine_Ridge.png; p. 21 UniversalImagesGroup/Getty Images; p. 23 Marquette University Archives, Bureau of Catholic Indian Missions Records, ID MUA_HRM_RCIS_02075; p. 25 https://upload.wikimedia.org/wikipedia/commons/9/98/Black_Elk.jpg; p. 27 E R DEGGINGER/Science Source/Getty Images; p. 28 Marquette University Archives, Bureau of Catholic Indian Missions Records, ID MUA_HRM_RCIS_00039; p. 29 welcomia/Shutterstock.com.

Library of Congress Cataloging-in-Publication Data

Coleman, Miriam, author.
 The life of Black Elk / Miriam Coleman.
     pages cm. — (Native American biographies)
 Includes bibliographical references and index.
 ISBN 978-1-5081-4826-5 (pbk.)
 ISBN 978-1-5081-4779-4 (6 pack)
 ISBN 978-1-5081-4814-2 (library binding)
 1. Black Elk, 1863-1950—Juvenile literature. 2. Oglala Indians—Biography—Juvenile literature. I. Title.
 E99.O3B53 2016
 978.0049752440092—dc23
 [B]
                                    2015027145

Manufactured in the United States of America

CPSIA Compliance Information: Batch #BS16PK: For Further Information contact Rosen Publishing, New York, New York at 1-800-237-9932

CONTENTS

A SACRED VISION

When Black Elk was just nine years old, he had a vision that changed his life. Lying ill in his parents' **tepee**, he dreamed of horses, thunder, and six grandfathers who shared special knowledge of the spirit world. When he awoke, Black Elk was no longer sick, but he would never be the same.

In his vision, the grandfathers showed Black Elk how he could help his people by bringing them back into the "sacred hoop" that held them together. Over the course of his life, Black Elk was part of many important events for his people, including their victory at the Battle of the Little Bighorn and the terrible **massacre** at Wounded Knee Creek. The lessons from his vision stayed with him as he tried to keep the **culture** of his people alive through times of great change.

Black Elk's vision revealed to him that he had special powers he could use to help his people.

CHILDHOOD ON THE GREAT PLAINS

Black Elk was born in December 1863 on the Little Powder River, in what is now the state of Wyoming. His family was Oglala, which is one of the seven tribes of the Lakota people. His father, grandfather, and great-grandfather were all named Black Elk. His father was a **medicine man**, as were his grandfather and several uncles.

When Black Elk was young, the Lakota people lived a **nomadic** lifestyle. Black Elk spent his childhood hunting and camping throughout the western part of Lakota territory as the group followed bison herds. As a boy, he learned to fish and hunt with a bow and arrow, and he played war games with friends. They often tried to knock each other off horses.

According to the Lakota way of keeping time, Black Elk was born in the "Winter When the Four Crows Were Killed on Tongue River."

THE GREAT SIOUX NATION

THE LAKOTAS ARE PART OF A LARGER GROUP OF TRIBES CALLED THE GREAT SIOUX NATION. THEY ONCE LIVED IN MINNESOTA, WHERE THEY HUNTED SMALL GAME AND HARVESTED WILD RICE, BUT THEY OFTEN CLASHED WITH THEIR NEIGHBORS, THE OJIBWA. BY THE 1700S, EUROPEANS INTRODUCED HORSES TO THE LAKOTAS, WHICH ALLOWED THEM TO HUNT BISON. FOLLOWING BISON HERDS THEN BECAME A WAY OF LIFE FOR THE LAKOTAS, WHO MOVED INTO WISCONSIN, IOWA, AND THE DAKOTAS. LAKOTAS ARE COMMONLY CALLED SIOUX IN ENGLISH. THAT NAME, WHICH MEANS "SNAKELIKE ONES," WAS ORIGINALLY GIVEN TO THEM BY THEIR ENEMIES, THE OJIBWA.

THE BATTLE OF THE LITTLE BIGHORN

Black Elk and his band spent many summers camping and hunting along creeks in the Black Hills, which are mountains sacred to the Lakotas. Trouble was brewing, however. "Wasichus," or white people, under the protection of the U.S. Army, came into the Black Hills looking for gold. In 1876, Black Elk's band joined other tribes, including the Cheyenne, in forming a village along Montana's Little Bighorn River. They were led by the great chief Sitting Bull.

On June 25, Lieutenant Colonel George Armstrong Custer led an attack on the village. Thousands of Lakota and Cheyenne warriors defended the village, killing Custer and wiping out his troops. Black Elk, who was 12 years old, joined in the fighting. He even took his first scalp from a soldier he shot. This was a mark of great honor among Lakota men.

Lieutenant Colonel
George Armstrong Custer

FORT LARAMIE TREATY

IN 1868, THE U.S. GOVERNMENT SIGNED A TREATY WITH LAKOTA LEADERS AT FORT LARAMIE IN PRESENT-DAY WYOMING. IN RETURN FOR PEACE BETWEEN WHITES AND THE LAKOTAS, THE TREATY PROMISED THERE WOULD NEVER BE WHITE SETTLEMENT IN THE BLACK HILLS, WHICH WOULD BELONG TO THE LAKOTAS FOREVER. IN 1874, HOWEVER, WHITE **PROSPECTORS** FOUND GOLD IN THE BLACK HILLS, AND THE U.S. ARMY MOVED IN TO PROTECT THE MINERS. THE TREATY ALSO ENCOURAGED THE LAKOTAS TO SETTLE ONTO **RESERVATIONS**, WHICH COMPLETELY ALTERED THEIR WAY OF LIFE. THE LAKOTAS WHO REFUSED TO SETTLE ON RESERVATIONS WERE DECLARED ENEMIES OF THE UNITED STATES.

Historians believe the Lakota and Cheyenne village's population before the Battle of the Little Bighorn was around 8,000 people. Anywhere from 1,500 to 1,800 of them were warriors.

ESCAPE TO GRANDMOTHER'S LAND

The feeling of victory from the Battle of the Little Bighorn didn't last long, as more soldiers came into the Black Hills to fight the native people. Many Lakotas abandoned the struggle and went to live on the reservations, but Black Elk's band chose to keep moving. The soldiers continued to attack, and a harsh, snowy winter made it hard to find food. Eventually, the United States took the Black Hills from the Lakota people.

Driven from the land they loved, Black Elk's band traveled north to join relatives who had already escaped to Canada. They called the country Grandmother's Land. Bison were plentiful there, and life was easier at first. However, Black Elk, who was 15, often thought of his vision and his duty to bring his people back together.

During the harsh winter in Grandmother's Land, Black Elk and his people were starving. Black Elk had a vision that told him where to find bison, and he led his people there. They hunted and killed eight bison, which likely saved them from starvation.

BRINGING THE HORSE DANCE TO LIFE

Black Elk's family returned home from Canada after about two years in the North. Black Elk was 17 now, and he felt the power his vision gave him was increasing. Although he was fearful of that power, he finally revealed his vision to a medicine man named Black Road.

Black Road told him he needed to perform the horse dance from his vision in front of his people. Grand preparations were made, including teams of painted horses and riders, six old men to play the six grandfathers, and a tepee painted with scenes from Black Elk's vision. Black Elk even taught the men the songs he heard in his vision. From that moment, he became a medicine man whose duty was to heal the sick among his people.

MOVING TO THE PINE RIDGE RESERVATION

IN DECEMBER 1881, WHEN BLACK ELK WAS 18, HE MOVED TO THE PINE RIDGE AGENCY, WHICH WAS THE RESERVATION THE GOVERNMENT SET UP FOR THE OGLALAS IN SOUTH DAKOTA. HE WAS SADDENED BY HOW UNHAPPY HIS PEOPLE SEEMED. THEY LIVED IN SMALL LOG HOUSES AND WERE REMOVED FROM THE LIFE THEY HAD ONCE KNOWN. YET BLACK ELK WAS DETERMINED TO HELP THE OGLALAS, AS HIS VISION ORDERED HIM TO. HE PERFORMED TRADITIONAL CEREMONIES TO TRY TO MAKE LIFE BETTER AND HEALING **RITUALS** TO CURE THE SICK.

TEPEE DETAIL

Drawings on the outside of a tepee were very symbolic.
This is an example of images painted on a Lakota tepee.

THE WILD WEST SHOW

In 1886, when Black Elk was about 23 years old, he left Pine Ridge to see the world and learn more about the ways of the Wasichus. Along with Native Americans from different tribes, Black Elk joined Buffalo Bill Cody's Wild West show. The show traveled by train from Nebraska all the way across the country to New York City. Once there, he performed traditional dances in shows at Madison Square Garden for several months.

In March 1887, Black Elk joined Buffalo Bill and his cast on board a steamship bound for England. The journey took more than two weeks. The show was very popular and traveled around the country. As one of the best dancers in the group, Black Elk was chosen to perform for Queen Victoria.

This 1889 poster advertises Buffalo Bill's Wild West show, using imagery commonly associated with the American West. The advertisement promises showgoers an appearance by Buffalo Bill, as well as scenes from "actual" Native American life, such as war dances and horse-riding skills.

BUFFALO BILL

WILLIAM F. CODY, KNOWN AS BUFFALO BILL, WAS A LEGENDARY WESTERN SHOWMAN. BORN IN IOWA IN 1846, CODY SPENT HIS EARLY YEARS RIDING FOR THE PONY EXPRESS, MINING FOR GOLD, AND SERVING AS AN ARMY SCOUT. HE EARNED HIS NICKNAME FROM HIS EXCELLENT BUFFALO HUNTING SKILLS. A NATURAL SHOWMAN, CODY STARRED IN HIS FIRST STAGE PLAY IN 1872. IN 1883, HE DEVELOPED BUFFALO BILL'S WILD WEST SHOW. THE OUTDOOR SHOW BROUGHT A TASTE OF FRONTIER LIFE TO THE WORLD, WITH COWBOYS PERFORMING ROPE TRICKS, STAGED BATTLES, AND LIVE ANIMALS, INCLUDING BUFFALO AND ELK. IT RAN FOR ALMOST THREE DECADES.

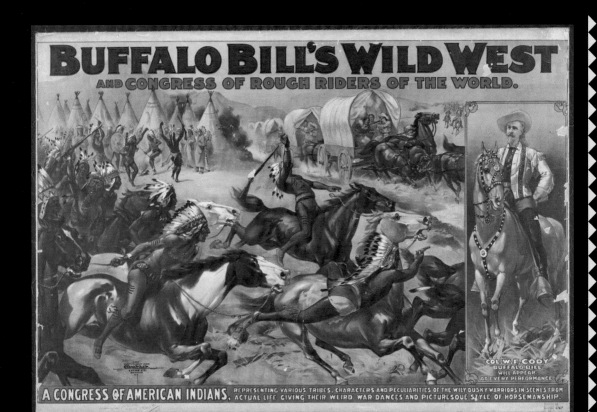

TRAVELS IN EUROPE

Black Elk became separated from Buffalo Bill's group just as they were about to return home to the United States. He joined another show run by a man called Mexican Joe. Black Elk traveled with this show through France, Italy, and Germany. As he traveled through Europe, he wrote letters home.

After two years in Europe, Black Elk became too ill to perform in the show, and he longed to be back home. In Paris, he met up again with Buffalo Bill, who gave him a ticket back to America along with $90. That's about $2,400 in today's money. After a long trip back across the ocean, he was reunited with his parents at Pine Ridge Reservation. Having learned a little English during his travels, he took a job as a store clerk.

Black Elk, left, is pictured here in 1887. He's dressed for Buffalo Bill's Wild West show.

THE GHOST DANCE

Life on the reservation was hard. The Lakotas suffered from **famine**, poverty, and hunger while the government failed to deliver promised food and supplies. Black Elk worried for his people. Soon after he returned, he learned of the Ghost Dance movement. Followers of this religious movement believed in a vision that said performing Ghost Dance ceremonies would bring **deceased** Native Americans back to life and make whites disappear forever. Many Lakotas followed this movement.

Black Elk went to see a Ghost Dance ceremony that was performed at Pine Ridge. He was shocked to find that many parts of the ritual matched what he had seen in his vision. He joined in and soon became a leader of the Ghost Dance, which he believed would help him bring his people back into the sacred hoop.

This illustration, which was created in 1890, shows one artist's idea of what a Ghost Dance ceremony may have been like.

WOVOKA'S VISION

IN 1889, A MAN NAMED WOVOKA FROM THE PAIUTE TRIBE IN NEVADA HAD A VISION THAT BECAME THE HEART OF THE GHOST DANCE MOVEMENT. WOVOKA'S MESSAGE SPREAD TO MANY TRIBES ACROSS THE WEST. THEY BELIEVED IF THEY COOPERATED WITH OTHER TRIBES AND PERFORMED THE GHOST DANCE RITUAL THAT WOVOKA SAW IN HIS VISION, IT WOULD BRING BACK THE PAIUTES' TRADITIONAL WAYS OF LIFE. ANCESTORS WOULD RETURN FROM THE DEAD, BISON WOULD RETURN TO THE PLAINS, AND WHITE PEOPLE WOULD DISAPPEAR, AS THOUGH THE TROUBLES THEY BROUGHT HAD JUST BEEN A BAD DREAM.

MASSACRE AT WOUNDED KNEE

In December 1890, a band of Miniconjou Lakotas was stopped by the U.S. Army at Wounded Knee Creek in South Dakota. The soldiers searched the Lakotas for weapons, which they took away. A medicine man began the Ghost Dance, and warriors in the group joined him. Army soldiers believed this was an act of war. During the commotion that followed, a Lakota man shot and killed a white soldier. Troops quickly began firing at the Lakotas, who grabbed their guns and fired back.

Black Elk was nearby when he heard the shooting. He and others rode over to help. They drove away and killed some of the soldiers, and they helped Lakota women and children escape. When the fighting stopped, Black Elk saw the terrible damage that had been done. The soldiers killed more than 250 Lakota men, women, and children.

OUTLAWING NATIVE TRADITIONS

BY 1890, THE U.S. GOVERNMENT HAD ALREADY OUTLAWED LAKOTA RITUALS SUCH AS THE SUN DANCE AND DISCOURAGED OTHER TRADITIONAL PRACTICES. WHEN THE GHOST DANCE MOVEMENT CAME TO THE LAKOTAS, IT FRIGHTENED THEIR WHITE NEIGHBORS, WHO THOUGHT IT MEANT THE LAKOTAS WERE PREPARING FOR WAR. FEDERAL AGENTS ORDERED THE DANCING TO STOP, AND THE ARMY CAME TO ARREST TRIBAL LEADERS. THE GHOST DANCE MOVEMENT DIED AMONG THE LAKOTAS AFTER THE HORRIFIC EVENTS AT WOUNDED KNEE CREEK.

The Battle of Wounded Knee is seen by many as symbolic of the United States' poor treatment of Native American groups.

FINDING CATHOLICISM

For some time after the Wounded Knee massacre, Black Elk turned away from the ways of the Wasichus because they had caused so much pain to his people. In his later life, Black Elk said of Wounded Knee, "A people's dream died there." He doubted the power of his vision. However, he continued practicing traditional healing for several more years.

Eventually, Black Elk became interested in Catholicism. In December 1904, he converted to Catholicism and was **baptized** as Nicholas Black Elk. He soon became a devoted member of the church, helping the priests on the reservation and leading services in Lakota. He also served as a missionary to other tribes in Wyoming and Nebraska, convincing at least 400 others to convert to Catholicism.

Black Elk (bottom row, first on the left) poses for a picture with officers of the Catholic Sioux Congress, missionaries, and church leaders at the Pine Ridge Indian Reservation in 1920.

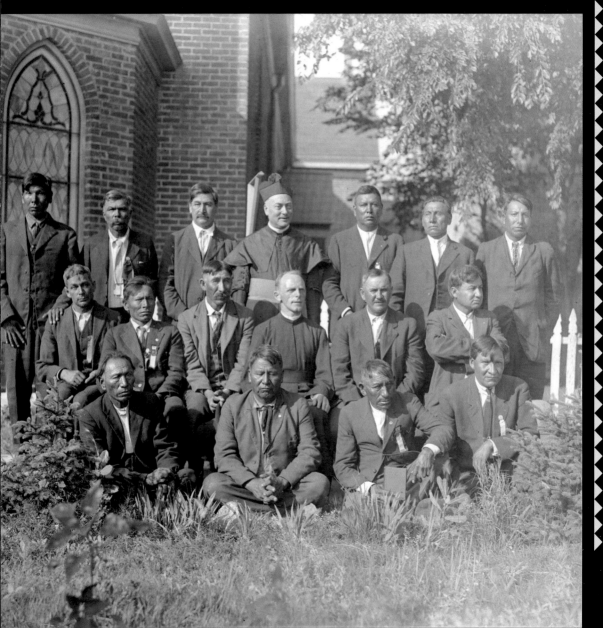

FAMILY LIFE

In 1892, when Black Elk was 28 years old, he married Katie War Bonnet. Together they had three sons: Never Showed Off (who was born in 1893 and later **christened** as William), Good Voice Star (who was born in 1895 and christened as John), and Benjamin (born in 1899). Sadly, William died around 1897, Katie died around 1903, and John died in 1909.

In 1906, Black Elk married Anna Brings White, a widow with a five-year-old daughter. Black Elk and Anna had two children—a daughter named Lucy, who was born that same year, and a son named Nick Jr. By the time Black Elk was an old man, he had a close family of grandchildren around him. He always encouraged his children and grandchildren to become educated, and they worked to preserve their grandfather's **legacy**.

This picture shows Black Elk and his family around 1910. Having converted to Catholicism, he no longer wears traditional Lakota clothing.

BLACK ELK SPEAKS

In 1930, when Black Elk was 67, a poet from Nebraska named John Neihardt came to visit him. Neihardt wanted to talk with someone who had witnessed the great events in Lakota history, but he became even more interested in Black Elk himself. He spent many days interviewing Black Elk about his life. Black Elk's son, Ben Black Elk, translated his father's words from the Lakota language. Neihardt published Black Elk's story in a book called *Black Elk Speaks*.

Black Elk felt a connection with the poet. He named Neihardt "Flaming Rainbow" and adopted him and his daughters into the Oglala tribe. Black Elk now believed that sharing his story with Neihardt was his way to help the old Lakota ways live on.

BOOK CONTROVERSY

BLACK ELK SPEAKS WAS A WORLDWIDE SUCCESS, BUT NOT WITHOUT **CONTROVERSY**. WHILE THE BOOK IS POPULAR AMONG NONNATIVE AUDIENCES, MANY NATIVE PEOPLE, ESPECIALLY LAKOTAS, HAVE SAID IT'S NOT AN ACCURATE REPRESENTATION OF THEIR TRADITIONAL WAYS OF LIFE. THEY FEEL NEIHARDT MAY HAVE CHANGED SOME PARTS OF BLACK ELK'S STORY IN ORDER TO APPEAL TO A NONNATIVE AUDIENCE. ALSO, CERTAIN IDEAS OR CONCEPTS MAY NOT HAVE BEEN TRANSLATED ACCURATELY FROM BLACK ELK'S LANGUAGE INTO ENGLISH.

Black Elk may have performed Lakota rituals for Neihardt at Harney Peak, which is pictured here.

BLACK ELK'S LEGACY

Black Elk kept in contact with Neihardt for many years after *Black Elk Speaks* was published in 1932. The two worked together on another book about Lakota history. Black Elk also spoke with another writer, Joseph Eppes Brown, about Lakota rituals for a book called *The Sacred Pipe*. In addition, he joined in the

Sioux Indian Pageant every summer, where he performed traditional Lakota rituals for tourists and continued to help others understand Native American religion.

Black Elk died of **tuberculosis** in Manderson, South Dakota, in 1950 at the age of 87. His vision and his story have continued to inspire generations of people. By sharing his vision with the world, he offered a unique window into Lakota history and beliefs, as well as a way to preserve his people's traditions.

Black Elk died in August 1950 on the Pine Ridge Indian Reservation in South Dakota. This picture shows land in the northern portion of the reservation.

TIMELINE OF BLACK ELK'S LIFE

1863 Black Elk is born.

1864 White prospectors open the Bozeman Trail into the Montana goldfields, cutting through the Lakotas' best hunting grounds. This sets off decades of conflict as the Lakotas respond by attacking the wagon trains of white settlers.

1868 The U.S. government signs the Fort Laramie Treaty, promising the Black Hills to the Lakotas forever.

1874 White prospectors find gold in the Black Hills.

1876 A band of Lakota and Cheyenne warriors defeats Custer and his army at the Battle of the Little Bighorn.

1881 Black Elk performs the horse dance from his vision and becomes a medicine man.

DECEMBER 1881 Black Elk moves to the Pine Ridge Reservation.

1886 Black Elk joins Buffalo Bill's Wild West show.

1889 Wovoka begins the Ghost Dance movement.

1890 U.S. Army soldiers kill more than 250 Lakota men, women, and children during the massacre at Wounded Knee Creek.

1892 Black Elk marries Katie War Bonnet.

1904 Black Elk converts to Catholicism.

1906 Black Elk marries Anna Brings White.

1930 John Neihardt comes to visit Black Elk.

1932 *Black Elk Speaks* is published.

AUGUST 1950 Black Elk dies in Manderson, South Dakota.

GLOSSARY

baptize: To sprinkle someone with water to show that person's acceptance into the Christian faith.

christen: To give a Christian name when someone is baptized, which is a sign of being accepted into the Christian church.

controversy: A disagreement.

culture: The beliefs and ways of life of a group of people.

deceased: Dead.

famine: An extreme lack of food.

legacy: Something handed down by someone.

massacre: A brutal killing of people.

medicine man: Among North American Indians, a person believed to have magical powers of healing and of seeing into the future.

nomadic: Traveling from place to place.

prospector: A person who searches for valuable mineral deposits.

reservation: An area of land set aside by the U.S. government for Native Americans to live on.

ritual: A religious ceremony.

tepee: A portable, tent-like dwelling made of animal skins, cloth, or canvas.

tuberculosis: A deadly sickness that usually attacks the lungs, but can also spread to other parts of the body.

INDEX

WEBSITES

Due to the changing nature of Internet links, PowerKids Press has developed an online list of websites related to the subject of this book. This site is updated regularly. Please use this link to access the list: www.powerkidslinks.com/natv/belk